Tomboy of the Air

Daredevil Pilot Blanche Stuart Scott

BY JULIE CUMMINS

HarperCollins*Publishers*

Special thanks and gratitude to the following people
who helped Blanche's story take flight

Kirk House, Glenn H. Curtiss Museum, Hammondsport, New York
William Hooper, New England Air Museum, Windsor Locks, Connecticut
E. Louise Pruitt, Willys-Overland Knight Registry, Batavia, Illinois
Shirley Iversen, Local History Division, Rochester Public Library, New York

Tomboy of the Air
Copyright © 2001 by Julie Cummins
All rights reserved. No part of this book may be used or reproduced in any
manner whatsoever without written permission except in the case of brief
quotations embodied in critical articles and reviews.
Printed in the United States of America.
For information address HarperCollins Children's Books, a division of
HarperCollins Publishers, 1350 Avenue of the Americas, New York, NY 10019.
www.harperchildrens.com

Library of Congress Cataloging-in-Publication Data
Cummins, Julie.
Tomboy of the air / Julie Cummins.
p.   cm.
Includes bibliographical references.
ISBN 0-06-029138-9—ISBN 0-06-029243-1 (lib. bdg.)
1. Scott, Blanche Stuart, 1886–1970—Juvenile literature.   2. Women air pilots—
United States—Biography—Juvenile literature.   [1. Scott, Blanche Stuart,
1886–1970.   2. Air pilots.   3. Women—Biography.]   I. Title.
TL540.S368 C85   2001   00-032009
[B]   CIP
AC

Typography by Stephanie Bart-Horvath
1   2   3   4   5   6   7   8   9   10
❖
First Edition

To Blair, who copiloted this book

Never publicity shy, Blanche was always ready to pose for photographers.

Contents

CHAPTER 1

Speed and Balance

E ven as a child, Blanche Stuart Scott was a daredevil. She was fascinated with activities that involved moving fast. "I always liked speed," she said, "and I had a very good sense of balance."[1] That spunk and those skills would play a major role in her life.

Blanche was an only child, and her parents indulged her tomboyish interests. Her father, John Stuart Scott, had made a fortune manufacturing a widely used patent medicine for horses. Blanche was his pride and joy, and he happily catered to her every whim. She won several medals for ice-skating, competing in long-distance events, and she was a sensation on a bicycle. She was determined to become an expert trick bike rider and later said, "I could always do any trick I ever saw done on a bike."[2] But after she smashed up her seventh bike, her father declared he would never buy her another. She badgered him with tantrums and tears, and the very next day he gave in to her pleas, this time for a car, and bought her a Cadillac. Blanche was off and going full speed ahead.

This turn-of-the-century scene of Main Street in Rochester, New York, shows the main modes of transportation: walking, carriages, bicycles, and trolleys.

Few of Blanche's antics would seem out of the ordinary except for the time when they happened: The year was 1902. At the turn of the century, automobiles were quite uncommon. The single-cylinder Cadillac Blanche's father bought her was one of only one hundred cars in Rochester, New York, where the Scotts lived. Streets were not paved, and driving a car was not something proper for any child to do, let alone a young girl! But Blanche was far from caring about being proper. At age thirteen, her reckless driving in the city startled the horses pulling carriages and the pedestrians trying to walk on the streets. She became such a nuisance and a danger, speeding around the city at thirty miles an hour, that the Rochester City Council called a special meeting. Hoping to keep the streets safe, they issued an emphatic statement: "Stop this child from driving a dangerous vehicle!"[3] But since there were no laws governing automobiles and driver's licenses didn't exist, their ultimatum had no effect on Blanche. Impulsive and adventurous by nature, she wasn't about to let any city officials slow her down, and she went chugging merrily on her way.

The city's problem, or problem child, disappeared in a few years when Blanche's father died and her mother, Belle, took over his business. She sent Blanche off to boarding school in New England, with

"Stop this child from driving a dangerous vehicle!"

high hopes that her daughter would become more ladylike and ready to take her place in society. Somehow, Blanche's disposition didn't fit that mold.

Blanche came by her pluck and daring honestly. Her ancestors were direct descendants of Pilgrims who came to America on the *Mayflower*. Relatives would shake their heads over Blanche's escapades and say, "She's so like Grandmother Scott!" The comments pleased Blanche no end, as Grandmother Scott was strictly a no-nonsense pioneer homemaker, who protected the family farm from intruders with a rifle—and she was a deadly shot.

All "dolled up" for her automobile trip across country, Blanche is wearing a fashionable touring outfit. The slogan "Over land in an Overland" is painted on the engine cover.

CHAPTER 2

Over Land in an Overland

A fter graduation, Blanche returned home. She didn't want to go to college, as her parents had wished, and she found life in Rochester dull. Instead, she headed to New York City, where she got a job at a time when women did not routinely work outside the home. It was even more unusual because of what Blanche was selling. She was an automobile salesperson, and she was very likely the first woman to be one.

Blanche was keen on making a name for herself. When she realized that most women knew nothing about automobiles and were not encouraged to know anything about them, let alone drive them, she seized the opportunity to change all that. She sent a letter to the Willys-Overland Motor Company suggesting that they sponsor her in a transcontinental driving trip, something she thought no woman had ever ventured to do.

The official purpose of the trip was "to interest women in the value of motor car driving, provide wonderful educational possibilities attending such a trip across the continent, and to promote the benefits of long-distance touring from a health standpoint."[1] The publicity would encourage women to drive, she argued, and prove that anyone, even a woman, could drive a car.

The deal was made, and freckle-faced, red-haired, five-foot-one Blanche set off on May 16, 1910, from New York City. Thousands of people lined Fifth Avenue to see the white-and-silver "Lady Overland" begin a historic trip from the Atlantic to the Pacific.

Factory-manufactured cars had very basic equipment. By comparison, the Lady Overland was a fancy car. It was a 25-horsepower stock model 38 that sold for one thousand dollars. It had four cylinders, two spare tires, water bottles, two five-gallon cans containing gas and oil, acetylene lamps for night driving, and a cylinder of compressed air in case of a flat. The rear seat was removed to put in a large wooden box that served as a trunk, carrying clothing, tools, and spare parts. The trunk was a novelty, because early cars were not designed with trunks. People exclaimed over it in every town. Several years later, a trunk became a standard part of car design.[2]

Mayor William J. Gaynor officiated as Blanche took off from Manhattan, with cheering photographers knocking themselves out taking pictures. As a special symbol of the historic event to come, the mayor presented Blanche with a bottle of water from the Atlantic Ocean for her to pour into the Pacific, signifying the transcontinental achievement.

Blanche was accompanied by Amy Phillips, a newspaperwoman. Even though she did not know how to drive, Amy's job was to create a record of the trip, which would be turned into an advertising handout.

Painted in large letters on both sides of the car was the message THE CAR, THE GIRL AND THE WIDE, WIDE WORLD—NEW YORK TO SAN FRANCISCO. Hard rains plagued the beginning days of the trip, prompting Blanche to suggest their slogan should read "The Car, the Girl, and the Wet, Wet World."

After a week on the road, the rigors of the trip proved to be too much for Blanche's companion, and she was replaced by her sister Gertrude Phillips, also a journalist. They still had a long way to go, with unexpected challenges ahead.

All of the big newspapers reported their progress with great interest, running pages of photographs and stories every Sunday. Each night, Blanche sent a telegram to the Overland Company, telling them where she was, so each car agency could track her progress by moving a cardboard cutout of the car on a painted map in the dealer's window. Their arrival in each new city was greeted by city officials, fans, and members of the local automobile club, who escorted them to dinner as honored guests.

The cross-country route was not in a straight line, because Blanche drove from one Overland agency to the next, 175 in all, which created a zigzag course, doubling the actual miles from three

A map in an Overland car agency window in Cleveland, Ohio, marking Blanche's early progress in her trip. The arrow shows how far she had driven and how far she had to go!

E. Louise Pruitt, librarian of the Willys-Overland-Knight Registry's Collection

thousand to six thousand.

The trip was filled with hazards. Blanche described the situation this way: "You must realize that, those days, there were only 218 miles of paved roads, exclusive of cities, in the U.S. There weren't even any road maps for certain parts of the country, where cowpaths along the old Union Pacific [Railroad] were the only roads."[3]

As they approached Dayton, Ohio, they became trapped by a crowd of ten thousand excited people trying to see a unique flying spectacle at the Wright brothers' airfield. Wilbur and Orville Wright had captured public attention and made history. They built and flew the first powered heavier-than-air plane at Kitty Hawk, North Carolina, on December 17, 1903. The frenzied mob of people were there to see the marvel of what one headline described as TWO AIRPLANES IN

"anyone poking around in the clouds in a glorified kite had to be a nut ..."

Blanche is digging deep in the specially created trunk that held supplies for the long trip.

E. Louise Pruitt, librarian of the Willys-Overland-Knight Registry's Collection

FLIGHT OVER THE SAME FIELD AT THE SAME TIME. The pilots were Wilbur Wright and the Wright brothers' first student pilot. Blanche fumed over the delay, pronouncing that "anyone poking around in the clouds in a glorified kite had to be a nut . . . a complete and absolute idiot!"[4] Little did she realize she had just glimpsed her future. Within a few months, she would join the "crazy ones."

When Blanche reached the Rocky Mountains on her way to Lake Tahoe, an incredibly steep road brought the car to a stop. The Lady Overland simply couldn't make it up the grade. The two women resorted to a block and tackle—a leverage device that would pull the car slowly over the hump. Gertrude went up to the top of the hill to drive in a stake that would provide the hauling pivot. She came back white-faced and crying, claiming she had encountered an enormous wildcat. Blanche insisted it was just her companion's imagination, but she grabbed a gun from the car—a Colt .32—and took off, coming face-to-face with a large lynx. Panicking, and pointing the gun everywhere except at the wildcat, Blanche became elaborately polite, stared into the cat's eyes, and blurted, "How do you do?" Then she continued to mutter nice things, telling him how friendly and beautiful he was, all the while taking giant steps backward. When she reached the car, she jumped into the driver's seat, gunned the motor, and yelled to Gertrude, "This [darn] car just has to go over the grade!" And it did.[5]

A challenge of a different nature was the lack of bathroom facilities. An escort car preceded the Lady Overland by a mile or so, and rival car companies sent out their cars with reporters—all of them men—for days at a time to record any predicaments or problems. The two women couldn't risk the embarrassment of stopping the car and using the roadside as a bathroom, in case the men in the escort car might come racing back, thinking they were in trouble.

A drugstore window display in a small western town gave Blanche the idea for a solution to their problem. She bought a stomach pump with a wide funnel attached to a long hose. By cutting a hole in the floorboard of the car and inserting the pump and funnel, she created a portable potty, enabling her and Gertrude to drive all day without stopping. Blanche delighted in mystifying the reporters, who couldn't figure out how two women could drive all day without stopping. She answered them with the quip "cast-iron kidneys."[6]

The car's top speed was fifty miles an hour, reached by streaking across a hard-packed lake bed in Nevada. The greatest distance Blanche covered in one day was 260 miles, and the least distance was fourteen frustrating miles across a series of streams and uncharted rivers without bridges.

With grand ceremony, Blanche and Gertrude arrived in San Francisco on July 23, 1910. A street parade, a military band, newsmen, and the mayor welcomed Blanche on the completion of the historic coast-to-coast trip, which had taken ten weeks, with forty-two days of actual driving. To symbolize the transcontinental milestone, Blanche, with great fanfare, poured the presumed bottle of Atlantic water into the San Francisco reservoir, which merged with the Pacific. Typical of Blanche's craftiness was the real water story. When she arrived at the hotel and unpacked, the bottle of water, which had been widely publicized on the trip, was nowhere to be found. Blanche called the hotel busboy, who provided a small bottle, and plain old tap water became the ceremonial symbol. Blanche's quick thinking had saved the day and the event.

Where's Blanche in the midst of this cheering crowd? She's sitting in the Lady Overland, just right of center, on her arrival in San Francisco in front of the Ferry Building.

New England Air Museum, Borden Collection

Blanche and her flying instructor, Glenn Curtiss, whose stern look indicates how he felt about working with women, especially one with Blanche's temperament and wily ways. She was very likely the reason why Curtiss taught only one woman to fly—her. Blanche signed the photo with her nickname, Betty, noting, "I really don't feel as ugly as I look."

CHAPTER 3

Up in the Air

A n Overland car distributor in Southern California first sparked Blanche's interest in flying. Glenn Martin was a pioneer aviator himself. He had met Blanche during her car trip and seized the opportunity to make the first woman to drive across the continent also the first female airplane passenger. Blanche laughed at the idea of anyone being crazy enough to fly, but craziness and speed had always appealed to her.

When an Associated Press reporter arranged for her to ride in a two-seater plane for a news stunt, Blanche was both excited and scared. The exploit would make her the first woman passenger to fly in an airplane in the United States. She was thankful, though, when the scheme fell through because a severe windstorm the day before had demolished the plane; it was reduced to a heap of cloth, wires, and sticks. The fact that the flight hadn't taken place didn't keep the story from appearing in print anyway. To meet his deadline, the reporter had filed the story a day ahead of the scheduled takeoff, and it was published as if it happened. The story foreshadowed the news Blanche would make by flying.

Blanche thoroughly enjoyed the fame from her news-making automobile trip, but she was greatly disappointed when her arrival back in New York City by train went unnoticed—no bands, no hullabaloo. Adding to her chagrin was the discovery that another woman, Alice Ramsey, had made a cross-country automobile trip the year before her. Though the credit of being "first" slanted in Blanche's favor because she had driven the entire distance herself and had made her own repairs, which Ramsey had not, it was a letdown.

When she was offered a job as head of a driving school, she was ready to accept. Then Frank Tipton, a press agent for the Glenn Curtiss Flying Exhibition Company, suggested that she could promote Curtiss aircraft in the same way that she had promoted Overland cars. Having read the newspaper story, he made her an offer: "Since you already know the great exhilaration of flying, how would you like to learn to fly?"[1]

Not wanting to risk the AP newsman's job by revealing the true story, Blanche stammered, "Maybe you've got something there. It could very well be a wonderful idea!" Three days later, she signed a contract to join the Curtiss team.[2]

Aviation was just literally getting off the ground as man's attempts to fly were in the very beginning stages. Rivalry was intense between the Wright brothers and Glenn Curtiss to obtain patents for airplane designs. Both competitors used exhibition teams to raise money to continue their experiments in building and designing airplanes.[3] The flying machines were a huge novelty and drew large crowds and big money wherever they were flown. Since no woman had ever piloted a plane, Tipton perceived that adding Blanche to the Curtiss team would be real one-upmanship.

Curtiss was furious that the manager of his flying team, Jerome Fanciulli, had signed Blanche to a contract while he was out of the country. He didn't like the idea of a woman on his team, and he didn't want to teach a girl to fly. When Blanche arrived in Hammondsport, in the Finger Lakes region of New York, she received a frosty reception. Though Curtiss had a progressive attitude about aviation, he, like most men of his day, felt a woman's place was on the ground, in the home, and not in the air. He felt caught between the advantage of good publicity about training the first woman

"Here I am, and I have a contract."

to fly and the prospect of adverse publicity if a female had a plane accident. Curtiss told her that if she were killed or injured while flying, it would set aviation back twenty years! In response to his resistance, Blanche smiled and said, "Here I am, and I have a contract."[4]

Reluctantly, Curtiss began training Blanche to fly in a single-seat biplane. Known as the "Curtiss Pusher," the biplane looked like a huge tricycle with transparent wings and a propeller in the rear. The pilot sat in front on a seat out in the open, with the four-cylinder engine positioned midway between the wings and directly behind the pilot's seat. If the plane crashed, which was a real possibility, the motor could break loose and decapitate the pilot. No wonder the seat was named the "undertaker's chair." As Blanche explained, "We had to balance the plane in flight and during the banks the same as when you ride a bicycle, by body control."[5]

Blanche's initial lessons consisted of taxiing the plane up and down the grass field while Curtiss ran along beside her, shouting instructions. The "grass-cutting" technique was a simple way of becoming familiar with the controls and getting a feel for the plane without taking off. She would taxi to one end of the field and a mechanic would turn the plane around so that she could taxi back in the opposite direction.

To keep the plane on the ground, a block of wood was wedged under the foot throttle, which prevented the engine from getting enough fuel to lift the plane high enough to become airborne.

Blanche was fashionably dressed for her first flying lesson. Her becoming tailored suit had an ankle-length pleated skirt with about four yards of material at the hemline. That was her first problem: The grass-cutting exercises created enough wind to blow her skirt up over her head.

"Women's future in the air was assisted by a mechanic who came riding down the field on his bicycle. He calmly reached down, unhooked

Blanche turning the propeller prior to takeoff

the clips he had on his trouser legs, strode over to the plane and silently handed them to me. I gathered as much of my skirt as possible around each ankle and clamped the clips. I was ready," Blanche said.[6]

After four days of taxiing and grass-cutting exercises, a gust of wind caught the plane and lifted it into the air. Blanche landed without any damage to the plane, but she had just experienced her first taste of the sensation of flying. "I soared to the dizzying height of 25 feet. It seemed like a hundred! My only concern was a desperate desire to land the plane upright and intact. I had tasted blood and from now on there was no holding me."[7]

The next step in learning to fly was to progress from grass-cutting maneuvers to "hopping"—swooping into the air for a few feet and coming back down. During the time that Blanche continued her hopping exercises, an amusing incident occurred. Financial aid was critical to aviation pioneers in order to underwrite the costs of their experimentation. Mabel Bell, the wife of Alexander Graham Bell, the famous inventor of the telephone in 1876, was quietly backing some of Curtiss's experiments. She supplied the money, but her husband handled the business matters. Dr. Bell sent two men as consultants to Curtiss. One day, when a particular situation arose, a big discussion took place about sending a three-hundred-word telegram to Dr. Bell, who was in Canada. It

"I soared to the dizzying height of 25 feet."

would be expensive. Blanche suggested they write out the questions and put in a long-distance phone call to Bell, which would take less time than a telegram, would cost less, and would give them the answers immediately. The shocking response was that Dr. Bell said phones were a darned nuisance and he wouldn't have one in his house![8]

During her training, Blanche lived with the Curtiss family in Hammondsport. Their house was not within walking distance of the airfield. Blanche prodded Curtiss, who also owned a motorcycle business, to loan her a motorcycle for going back and forth. He conceded and gave her one, but it was heavy and not equipped to stand upright in a parked position. Since Blanche was short, her legs didn't reach the ground when she stopped to get off. She solved her predicament by riding up to the plane hangar, putting her hand on the wall, and dismounting. When she rode back to the house, she would just fall off onto the soft lawn.

Many famous people came to see Curtiss. One day, the internationally known flier Alberto Santos-Dumont was sitting with Curtiss on the front porch when Blanche rode up. She didn't want to appear undignified in front of such a famous person by falling off the motorcycle, so she headed for the big tree in front of the house. She planned to balance against it and gracefully get off the cycle, but in her excitement she accelerated, instead of cutting the motor. "I hit the tree head on, went head over heels over the handlebars and landed right in front of the porch. Both men rushed to reach me, and

Mr. Santos-Dumont got there first. He turned to Mr. Curtiss and in his delightful French accent said, 'The little lady does not need to have an aeroplane to fly, she flies by herself!' "[9]

As Blanche continued her hopping, she became more and more eager to get off the ground. "Each day I hopped higher and higher into the air. Oh, how I wanted to go up, really fly into the air and circle the field."[10]

National Air and Space Museum, Smithsonian Institution (SI neg. no. 85-14221)

The Curtiss Pusher that Blanche first flew looked like a giant tricycle with huge wings.

It finally happened on September 2, 1910. "That day, I took-off, supposedly for just a hop down the field, and went sailing into the air. I went up to about 150 feet, made two turns over the field and landed with ease. It was my first real solo flight."[11] Blanche had just made history. She was the first woman to fly in the United States!

From his office, Curtiss saw her flying the plane and was astonished, and furious. Seeing that his attempts to keep Blanche on the ground had failed, "His jaw fell open. He thought, she's flying—she'll crash—she'll ruin me!"[12] Curtiss was afraid she had endangered the reputation of his flying school. When Blanche landed the plane gently and climbed out, she smiled and said demurely, "Something must have happened to that throttle block."[13]

Many accounts of her flight suggest that Blanche had deliberately removed the throttle block, despite Curtiss's instructions not to. But the Aeronautical Society of America dismissed her feat as accidental. It credited Bessica Raiche as the first American woman aviator. Raiche *announced* that she would fly on Long Island on September 16—and she did. Yet she did not soar as long or as high as Blanche had. Raiche herself felt there was no question about who was first. "Blanche deserved the recognition,"[14] she said candidly.

Intentional or accidental, Blanche's accomplishment was significant not only in the records of flying but also in the women's rights movement. At the time, women were expected to get married and have children. Only certain refined professions, such as teaching, were open to them if they were unmarried. Equally repressive was the fact that women did not have the right to vote until 1920, when the Nineteenth Amendment to the Constitution was passed.

Having succeeded at soloing, Blanche continued to take off

successfully, control the plane in the air, and land. The one part where she had difficulty was banking the plane in a turn. She was afraid that when the plane tipped, it would slide to the ground. "Mr. Curtiss kept trying to explain and impress on me why banking was so important. That's what the ailerons are for, all the aviators kept telling me."[15] The hinged flaps on the wings allowed the plane to bank and turn. Blanche's fear of banking was the cause of her first accident. As she was flying over Keuka Lake, she banked too far at a low altitude, dipped the left wing into the water, and the plane slid into the lake, crumpling the wing and breaking Blanche's ankle. The incident left her far from overcoming her fear of banking.

Nevertheless, she was zealous in wanting to fly publicly and began to beg Curtiss to allow her to join his exhibition team. A month after her historic flight, he told her she was going along to Chicago for the National Air Meet, where she would make her first public flight. It would have happened if not for Mrs. Curtiss.

Warm and friendly, Mrs. Lena Curtiss had a strong sense of public relations and good business skills, which fostered the growth of the Curtiss business, but it was her regard for others and her remarkable memory that kept Blanche from flying in her first air show. She remembered Blanche's accident and that Blanche had confessed a fear of flying over water when she first began her lessons by Lake Keuka. Mrs. Curtiss insisted that flying in the Chicago meet over Lake Michigan would make Blanche too anxious. Blanche saw the show,

Posed and poised at the controls, Blanche always had onlookers when she was ready for takeoff.

but from the ground, as a spectator in the audience.

Blanche's chance finally came a few weeks later when Curtiss announced she would be a co-exhibitor with Bud Mars in Fort Wayne, Indiana. Mars was famous, and she hoped fame would find her, too, as she was at last a member of Curtiss's exhibition team. But Blanche's excitement over her first meet was dampened by a dose of reality when she saw the field in Fort Wayne. It was a combination one-mile racetrack and fairgrounds, where a county fair had been held the week before. A demonstration of plowing equipment had churned the infield, where the planes were to take off, into ruts and trenches.

Brought in by railroad cars, the planes were assembled on the field. While they were designed to lift off and become airborne, they were not built to endure rough ground conditions of this kind.

Bud felt it was too dangerous to take off from the plowed-up infield, which left Blanche in a quandary. The Curtiss team had a remarkable safety record. If Blanche had a mishap, it would be a major setback not just for her but also for future women fliers and the Curtiss company. Yet the prospect of another disappointing delay was too much to bear. After failing to convince Bud that she could take off from the racetrack, which presented a serious hazard because a fence allowed only ten feet of clearance for the wings, Blanche persisted. She took off from the rutted field, jolting and bumping over the uneven ground. She flew eight circles around the infield and landed on the racetrack, with no mishaps. On October 23, 1910, she had made the first public flight in an airplane by a woman.

Blanche was overjoyed that she had made a second historic flight. As she walked off the field, she overheard two women talking about what they had just seen. They declared it was dull because there had been no accidents and no one had been killed. For the first time, Blanche realized that the public's eagerness to observe thrills provided by daredevil fliers included a morbid fascination, and it hit home hard. It was a blow to understand that some in the crowds came hoping to see crack-ups, accidents, and injuries.

Though it was unsettling to Blanche, she was determined to be an exhibition flier. It was an emotion of another kind that interrupted her plans—love. The press agent who had plotted the coast-to-coast fanfare for Blanche's cross-country automobile trip had definitely not forgotten her; quite the opposite, he had personal plans for her.

Blanche admired Harry Tuttle, knowing he had promoted her to the fullest. Since the automobile trip, they had kept in touch with each other. He offered one marriage proposal after another, but Blanche kept stalling, explaining that she had started something—flying—and that she owed it to herself and the people who had backed her to see it through.

"I was in love! Sweet Love!"

On the evening of her historic first public airplane flight by a woman, Blanche called Harry by telephone and he asked her to marry him. He said the feat proved that she'd accomplished enough. She took the night train to Detroit, and they were married the next day.

"I was in love! Sweet Love! Anything and everything was great! I agreed to give up everything and settle down in a housewifely routine, for which I was magnificently unprepared and temprementally [sic] unadaptable. Sweet dreams of youth! The rosy path stretches into a rose petaled eternity. How few realize that the path is rocky, difficult and somewhat like running the mile in a sea of soft marshmallows wearing hobnails."[16]

Blanche canceled her contract with Curtiss and the newlyweds set up housekeeping in Dayton, Ohio. Young, adventurous Blanche attempted to busy herself with domestic duties, but she was far from being ready to assume the placid, tranquil lifestyle of a typical married woman, who, in those days, did not have a career and did not step out of the role of the dutiful wife, especially to fly airplanes. Blanche found that the humdrum of playing bridge and socializing had grounded her in more ways than one.

"I discovered I was totally unsuited for the life of bridge, telephoning, socials and social visiting. The great big world was out there and there were things to be done that were more important than who trumped Charlie's ace or who fell into the punch bowl Saturday at the Country Club. The interests of Dayton society were a million light years from mine, I couldn't care less about bridging the gap."[17]

What kept tugging at Blanche was the urge to fly. She was a constant visitor to the Wright brothers' field in Dayton, watching them train others and longing to be part of the action. When other flying companies learned she had been released from her contract with Curtiss, they pursued her with offers. Eventually, Blanche couldn't resist.

"Each offer to fly was like a hot needle shoved into quivering flesh. There was an inescapable thrill and exhilaration in flying and being in the air. The attitudes and camaraderie of other flyers [*sic*] stirred in me feelings that I cannot truly describe. . . . My longing to be back in the air grew daily."[18]

Blanche disliked life with the social crowd in Dayton, and married life quickly became boring and uninteresting. She wanted to fly more than anything, but her husband wanted a homebody. The marriage lasted eight months. Blanche and Harry reached an amicable agreement, separated, and later divorced.

An aerial view of Blanche flying a Curtiss Pusher at Mineola, Long Island, in 1911.
Silhouetted against the sky, the length of the wings suggests how difficult it was to balance.

CHAPTER 4

Flying High and Far

F ree to fly again, Blanche wrote to the Wright brothers, but they wanted no part of a woman exhibition pilot. So in May 1911, Blanche went to Long Island, New York, where she signed a contract with Thomas Baldwin to fly at Mineola Field. He recognized the publicity value of having an attractive woman flying on his team. "The Captain," as Baldwin was dubbed, was fascinated with vehicles that transported man through the air. He'd begun his career as a balloonist and had obtained a license for balloon navigation. Next, he moved on to dirigibles, balloons with motors, which were, at the time, envisioned to be the ships of the future. The glamour of these large floating luxury motels diminished when several disasters turned the public against them.

Baldwin decided that planes were the up-and-coming vehicle, and so he learned how to fly. He built the first all-metal plane with fabric-covered wings. Aptly named the "Red Devil" because of the extreme difficulty in balancing a plane before stabilizers were invented, this plane challenged the skills of any pilot who flew it.

Many famous fliers were based at Mineola, and Blanche was proud to be associated with them. Doc Walden, a New York City dentist, who had built the first monoplane in the United States, was there. It was one of Doc's new designs that almost caused a disaster for Blanche.

In those early days of flying it was customary to maintain an altitude of between two hundred and three hundred feet, a distance that was dangerously close to the ground. That amount of altitude didn't allow for any space to maneuver. Blanche was up in the air on the day that Doc Walden made a maiden flight with a plane that he had just built. It was handsomely designed, except for one flaw. Doc had forgotten to build on a rudder, part of the steering mechanism. He was airborne, with no control of the plane at all, flopping and spinning around at a great rate. When Blanche realized that his plane was coming straight at her at a right angle, she knew she didn't have enough power to climb over the plane and that she was too close to the ground to go under it. She instinctively turned the plane around, reversed her direction, and landed, avoiding a midair collision.

On the ground, Blanche let loose with a temper tantrum, screaming, "Who let that murdering idiot loose in the air over this field? He ought to be locked up in an airtight room and the key thrown into the ocean!"[1]

No one was listening to Blanche. Instead, the spectators kept asking her, "How did you do it?" When she stopped ranting long enough to ask what they were talking about, the reply was, "No one has ever done that maneuver before—that turn is something new!" Blanche had made a hairpin turn, a steep vertical climb perpendicular to the ground, with a hard roll to the right of 180 degrees, an almost-impossible maneuver because of the sharpness of the turn. That same turn became famous when a World War I German ace pilot used it, and the maneuver was named the Immelman turn after him. Pilots still use the Immelman move today. It wouldn't be the first or last time that Blanche's quick thinking helped shape flying techniques.

By now, Blanche had solved the problem of what to wear while flying. The numerous petticoats for proper full-length dresses were unmanageable and hazardous, even when using bicycle clips. She had a New York City designer fashion a brown satin suit with baggy knee breeches. She wore the suit with high boots, a brown plush helmet with earmuffs, and gauntlets. This was daring attire for a woman at the time, but her full-cut "bloomers" with three petticoats stuffed inside were definitely suitable for flying.[2]

There was one other important item in Blanche's jaunty outfit. She was superstitious about an old red sweater, which buttoned down the front. She always wore this red sweater, believing it was "a symbol of a guardian angel who protected her from harm."[3] That guardian angel would be put to the test several times.

New England Air Museum, Scott Collection

LEFT: Blanche in her lucky red sweater and flying helmet

OPPOSITE: Dressed in her signature flying outfit with goggles, helmet, and specially designed bloomers, Blanche gets some last-minute advice.

In the summer of 1911, when not even a full year had passed since Blanche had made her historic liftoff, two women arrived at Mineola to learn to fly. Blanche did not know them, but her breakthrough into aviation paved the way for other women to follow. Matilde Moisant was the sister of Johnny Moisant, a famous exhibition flier. Though Matilde learned to fly and was scheduled to join an exhibition team, a terrible accident ended her flying career on April 14, 1912.[4] Harriet Quimby was the other woman who trained at Mineola, and she went on to become a famous female pilot. Blanche's path would cross Quimby's several times over the next year.

When Blanche soloed in 1910, licenses for pilots did not exist. By 1911, a French agency, the Federation Aeronautique Internationale, had begun to issue licenses, and many people expected the United States would do the same. The Aero Club of America stepped in and began to issue licenses. The club issued its first pilot's license, Number 1, to Glenn Curtiss on June 8, 1911. The intense competition between Curtiss and Orville Wright made the decision all the more significant.[5] The club began to forbid new pilots to fly without licenses, but they didn't require existing pilots to obtain them. The whole issue of licensing was controversial.

To her later regret, Blanche listened to those who argued against obtaining a license. "Glenn Curtiss told me not to bother to get one because they weren't worth the paper they were written on."[6] His opinion, shared by many experienced fliers, and the lack of any official government backing swayed Blanche into deciding not to obtain a license, a decision she would forever lament. It would cost her the claim of being the first *licensed* American woman pilot. Instead, Harriet Quimby snared that honor on August 1, 1911.[7]

For the rest of that summer of 1911, Blanche performed exhibition flying at state fairs, racetracks, carnivals, and anyplace where there was a crowd and an area to land. She loved the excitement of the events and the comradeship of the male pilots, who accepted her as one of them. An article in *The Saturday Evening Post* described the exhibition fliers as "a flock of adventurers [who] together convinced a skeptical but wide-eyed public that man could fly and, moreover cut some breathtaking didos [maneuvers] with his noisy fearsome toy. Early 'pinfeathered' birdmen they were and only a few survived the flimsy crates which they so recklessly looped over a thousand county fairgrounds."[8] The statement was not an exaggeration. There were 158 aviation fatalities in just four years, from 1908 to 1912.

For Blanche, the climax of that summer was when she appeared in a movie. Moving pictures, just like flying, were in a pioneer stage and were just beginning to be popular. Blanche was approached by the Champion Motion Picture Company of New Jersey, which saw an opportunity to make the first drama about flying at a time when the public was increasingly curious about aviation.

The movie would be filmed at Mineola Field and was called *The Aviator's Bride,* with Blanche playing the lead opposite the handsome pioneer flier Lee Hammond. Blanche loved every moment of the attention and being in the public eye again.

"In one of the scenes, I was to land and roll the plane right up to the camera for one of the early close-ups. This sounds simple. With those early planes with no brakes, it was almost impossible to plan the exact stopping spot. The halting point was the result of the terrain. We chose a rough and bumpy spot to slow us up and hazarded a guess as to exactly where the plane would stop. Let me set the scene further. Our cameraman was a short, plumpish Hungarian who looked ill at ease grinding the handle of his manually operated camera like a huge coffee mill. When I landed, the distance between the cameraman and where I hit the ground was a bit overshot. He stuck manfully to his job cranking away at the risk of his life. Luck and the braking quality of rough ground was on our side and we didn't collide but he got one of the closest close-ups in the history of motion pictures. It filled the entire screen and was probably the first giant economy sized close-up in film history."[9]

Public interest in flying generated a lot of news, and the motion picture brought increased attention and publicity for aviation. New planes, new records being made, and new developments in engineering and safety added to the focus on flying as hot news. Any accidents helped to sensationalize the daring aspects of flying. In an attempt to control crashes and disasters, fliers at Mineola were forbidden to fly beyond the limits of the airfield called Nassau Boulevard. The reason for this was the fear that if the pilots had to make an emergency landing, they might land on a rooftop or on a street, which would cause a panic. All of the New York City newspapers stationed a reporter at Mineola, anticipating a shocking crack-up or a thrilling mishap.

Blanche accidentally gave them a whopper of a story by losing her temper one day. When she arrived at the field, a disagreement with Captain Baldwin turned into verbal fireworks. She jumped into her Red Devil and took off. "What tripped off the shouting, I don't recall. I was mad, mad. I wanted to hit something and hitting the sky would have been only a short jump the way I felt. I got into my plane and instead of turning around to circle I went straight ahead, eyes front, absolutely blind with anger. When I did cool off I was over Central Islip. I had frequently visited the place and so it was easily recognized from the air. I had worked off my temper and decided to turn back. Meanwhile, back at the field, all was bedlam."[10]

Captain Baldwin and the other fliers, as well as the reporters, were worried. They saw Blanche take off and disappear into the blue sky, but when half an hour went by with no sign of her return, they began checking

"I was mad, mad. I wanted to hit something and hitting the sky would have been only a short jump the way I felt."

police stations to find out if anyone had reported an airplane crash. There was a frenzy of worry and excitement. The customary distance to fly from the Nassau Boulevard field to Garden City was two miles, not far enough to take that much time.

"My anger blacked out everything until I was over Central Islip. I had never considered that I had enough gas or how long the Red Devil would stay in the air. The motor was humming, the plane was eating the miles gracefully and I was regaining some of my shattered composure."[11]

When Blanche returned to the field, she was amazed to see a crowd of people, all of whom were looking up at the sky. As she landed, reporters rushed up to the plane to ask how far she had flown. When she answered that she had been over Central Islip, one of the men said, "Do you realize that's thirty miles out and thirty miles back!"[12] Headlines in the newspapers the next day proclaimed Blanche was the first woman to make a long-distance flight. She had set another record.

Navigating early planes like the Red Devil required intuitive skills. There were few instruments to depend upon; pilots had a speedometer and a land map, but apart

Just taking off, Blanche's plane makes quite a contrast to the early automobiles at the edge of the field.

National Air and Space Museum, Smithsonian Institution (SI neg. no. 75-5216)

from that, they had to depend on whatever landmarks they could pick up and follow, such as railroad tracks. Any long-distance flight could be further complicated by weather conditions and the limited capacity of fuel tanks. The risks and hazards of flying in those days were tremendous, but determined pilots were charting the future course of aviation.

Blanche was not spared from those risks. Twice during that eventful summer as she took off and became airborne, the wooden plane propeller shattered into small pieces. Both times she was able to land without any injury. She just assumed the accidents were the result of faulty manufacturing. Besides, she was okay—she had worn her lucky red sweater. It was some time later that she learned the truth.

The gas tanks were placed high on the back of the planes, with the openings level with the top wing surface. To fill the tanks, a mechanic had to lug the gas up a stepladder and pour it into them. On one occasion, when a mechanic left his wrench on the upper wing, it dropped into the propellers immediately on takeoff, causing them to shatter. Only after the second incident did Blanche somehow learn that the man had deliberately been sabotaging her plane, attempting to murder her! An investigation revealed the man was furious that Baldwin had not taught him to fly, as promised, and he resented that Blanche—a woman—was permitted to fly. The combination led to his malicious actions of destruction.[13]

For all of the curiosity and fascination with women aviators, as few as they were, there was a widespread public attitude that women should not be attempting such daredevil actions. People thought that the proper place for women was in the home. Blanche repeatedly defended women pilots to the men pilots who insisted that the public would never trust a woman to fly commercially. Her arguments for equal consideration for women pilots were dismissed by the men, but over time persistent women pilots would break down the gender barriers.

The third attempt on Blanche's life was made by a woman who claimed she was the widow of pilot Ralph Johnstone, who had been one of the original Wright brothers' exhibition team. One morning as Blanche was walking to her hangar, a tall, beautiful woman in a black cape walked up very close to her. She suddenly pulled out an ornate revolver and jammed it into Blanche's midsection. Blanche was quite startled and scared. She was being held at gunpoint. The field was almost deserted except for a mechanic and a flier, both some distance away. "To be shot so soon after breakfast on a bright and beautiful day wasn't on my list of 'Things To Get Done Today!'" Blanche said later. She figured her only chance was to talk the woman out of whatever she intended to do, and she boldly asked, "Would you please tell me what this foolishness is about?"[14]

The woman babbled on angrily, saying that Blanche had slandered her and her son, telling lies about them. By now, the flier, unaware of the situation, was getting close, and Blanche saw it was fellow pilot George Beatty. She tried to stall the woman until he was close enough to help. As the woman continued to rant about her son, Blanche yelled "GEORGE!" at the top of her lungs. "The woman turned instinctively. I immediately grabbed her wrist and shoved the gun high in the air. It glinted unmistakenly and George knew what it was. He came on at a dead run, grabbed the gun, wrenched it from her hand and shouted, 'What in the blue blazes is going on here?' I was as limp as a handful of wet spaghetti and could scarcely get out the words, 'This foolish woman wants to kill me.'"[15]

It was not Blanche who was telling lies; it was the woman. She wasn't really the widow of Ralph Johnstone, as she claimed. But she had been in love with him and wanted him to divorce his wife to marry her. He was killed in a plane crash before it could happen. Somehow, she had singled out Blanche as the object of her anger, knowing she had hung around the Wright brothers' field.

Shaken but unharmed, Blanche didn't forget the incident, but she had other thrills to think about.

Though the pilots at Mineola treated flying seriously, they weren't above inventing games for themselves. "We used to dive down on the trains that were crossing Long Island, and level off about 20 feet above them. We got a kick out of riding the buffets of air that hit us as each car passed under,"[16] Blanche said.

Their favorite game was Grab the Strut. The men who flew the Wright planes, which were two-seaters, came up with the scheme.

The expressions on their faces reflect the danger of the game as
Blanche and Lincoln Beachey play Grab the Strut.

Two pilots would go up together, one flying, the other as passenger. The object was for the pilot to maneuver the plane as wildly as possible to make the passenger pilot so nervous that he would reach out and grab the nearby strut to hold on. If that happened, he lost. Bets were always placed on the outcome.

One Saturday afternoon, George Beatty invited Blanche to join in the game. At an altitude of two hundred feet, he put the plane through every wiggle it could muster. Blanche was scared all right,

Looking determined, Blanche gets set for takeoff with pilot Glenn Martin behind her wearing a helmet. Months later they would put their heads together to design and test-pilot new planes.

but she gritted her teeth and sat quietly, which only encouraged George to go to further extremes. At that point, a checkered flag was waved at him from the ground, which meant "Come down immediately." When they landed, the crewman screamed at George, "What are you doing, taking a lady up and flying acrobatics? Do you want to scare her to death?" Amazed at the outburst, George replied, "Lady? Lady? That's no lady, that's Blanche Stuart Scott!"[17] It was a genuine tribute.

Those scares from flying shenanigans didn't unnerve Blanche as much as the annoyance of crank mail did. As her flying reputation grew, so did the phone calls and hate letters. For the most part, she didn't take them seriously, even the ones that prophesied when she would be killed. People accused her of blasphemy, saying if God had wanted her to fly, He would have given her wings. Others said it was indecent for a woman even to attempt to fly, a sentiment that many people had.

It was easier to shrug off the letters than to dismiss a face-to-face prediction of doom, which happened on her way to a meet. Blanche had forgotten her credentials and pass. Driving up to the field entrance, she explained who she was to the gatekeeper. He stared at her and dramatically pointed his finger at her, declaring, "You will be killed today! I dreamed last night that you were flying too low, hit the hangar and dashed into pieces."[18]

"Every cloud formation looked like a ghost dusting off a welcome mat...."

The encounter rattled Blanche more than she cared to admit. "I shall never forget that very uncomfortable afternoon in the air. No matter how I tried, I couldn't turn off an overactive imagination. Every cloud formation looked like a ghost dusting off a welcome mat with my name engraved on it. However, the hangar suffered no damage, the prophets of doom were confounded and there wasn't a single mishap. The gatekeeper's prophecy turned out to be a wonderful story to tell at parties."[19]

Miss Blanche Stuart Scott

Premier Woman Aviator of the World

Flying 80 H.P. Martin Biplane

Souvenir Los Angeles Aviation Meet

January 20-28 1912

CHAPTER 5

Circus in the Air

＝〰〰〰〰〰＝

Always on the alert for flying action, Blanche followed the newspaper stories about big air shows on the West Coast. She yearned to be in the midst of those exciting events, performing for large crowds. When a wire from the management of the Los Angeles meet arrived, inviting her to join them for their second big event, to be held in January 1912, she jumped at the chance. Blanche would be featured as a star attraction, along with Lincoln Beachey, one of the most famous U.S. pilots. Tremendous publicity fueled the public's enthusiasm. Huge headlines and posters promised spectacular daredevil stunts and hair-raising adventures. Crowds estimated at over 100,000 milled around the airfield each day. For one such turnout, a unique competition was held to keep the crowd's attention until the aerial feats began. It was a one-hundred-yard handicap race with a motorcycle, a man, a horse, an automobile, and a plane competing. The motorcycle won easily, followed by the man, horse, and car, with the plane showing a poor

This souvenir photo could be captioned "Hats Off to Blanche" as a group of men salute the "Premier Woman Aviator of the World."

New England Air Museum, Borden Collection

fifth. The contest entertained the crowd, but they knew the real show would be up in the air.

The airfield itself was good except for one thing: The landing strip ran parallel to the front of the grandstand but ended in a sheer drop of 150 feet into a canyon. Landing the planes, which had no brakes, was tricky enough, but there was no rail fence to stop a plane that kept rolling. At the time, small 50-horsepower engines fueled even the most powerful planes, and the planes' limited maneuverability added to the danger. There were elevators that moved the plane up and down, a wheel for steering, and ailerons for banking—but no brakes.

Because the small amount of horsepower limited how daring any

As Lincoln Beachey lands a biplane on a track in front of a packed grandstand, the spectators were close at hand. Not all landings were happy ones.

of the pilots could be, Beachey convinced Blanche to override her fear of banking and create a new stunt. By banking the plane as far as she could to one side and then banking sharply to the other side and repeating this action, she performed an aerial seesaw routine, which delighted the crowds.

The meet was a huge success in every way, including financially. Blanche was earning five thousand dollars a week! She had sizable expenses from transporting the plane, making repairs, and paying assistants. But when the average working man earned less than fifteen dollars a week and a quart of milk cost nine cents and a loaf of bread five cents, she was making big money!

That kind of financial success did not go unnoticed, and it caused increased interest in flying, particularly from one woman whom Blanche had never met. Ruth Law was the sister of Rodman Law, an experimenter in aerodynamics, who was way ahead of the times. "Miss Law wanted to know if I thought it would be profitable for her to learn to fly. I told her that if she wanted to take the chances necessary it could be as profitable for her as it had been for me. I also added that in addition to the money I really loved flying and enjoyed it. She then told me she'd been negotiating with the Wright Brothers about buying a plane, but they, like Glenn Curtiss, were reluctant to teach a woman to fly. Apparently they came to a meeting of the minds for shortly after this Ruth went to the old Wright Field at Dayton, Ohio."[1]

Just as Blanche was the only woman to be taught by Glenn Curtiss, Ruth Law became the only woman to be taught by the Wright brothers, and she became a noted woman flier.[2]

Following the huge popularity of the Los Angeles meet, plans were laid for the Great Western Aerial Circus in California, with Blanche and Beachey again as the feature attractions. While the financial backing and arrangements were being worked out, Blanche, Glenn Martin, and two airplane mechanics planned and built a couple of new plane models. Once a plane was completely built, Martin would take it up and test it. When he landed, the four of them would discuss what was right and what was wrong about the design, and then alterations were made. After that, Blanche would take the same plane up and offer her suggestions. Only after the testing and modifications were made to everyone's satisfaction were blueprints drawn up, and a new airplane was born. For her part, Blanche added "first woman test pilot" to her list of firsts.

The promoters of the Great Western Aerial Circus hired a top-notch publicist, Bill Pickens, to generate publicity as the circus traveled around California. He knew that it was the "stars," the name performers, who attracted people to the event, just as they attracted an audience for a play. So he billed Beachey as "the Greatest Daredevil Pilot in the World" and Blanche as "the Tomboy of the Air." Blanche was furious. She thought that being labeled a "tomboy" could ruin her public image and take away her dignity. She argued,

"You know what most people think about aviators. Their mental classification is that we are a rough, tough, bunch of uneducated idiots, who just happened to have enough skill and brainpower to move a highly tricky piece of expensive equipment through the air without killing either us or them. Heavens, I can read, write, spell. Fact is, as female education goes today, I would be considered well educated. My dignity means a lot to me even if I don't display it. I take a lot of trouble with my appearance and do my best to be seen only in attractive clothes."[3]

What changed Blanche's mind was when the promoter told her that she and Beachey would be featured on large posters plastered all over San Francisco and a dozen other towns down the California coast. Pickens also arranged for the railroads to run special excursions, and posters would be hung in all the railroad stations and hotels. Guaranteed that amount of publicity, Blanche was sold on being a "tomboy."

When the eight circus pilots saw the racetrack at the San Francisco meet, they were horrified. The track was an oval field, parallel to a rickety grandstand, with an open ditch bisecting it across the middle. That ditch cut the landing strip by two-thirds, making it too short to land safely. Without any brakes on the planes, the pilots had to come to a complete stop when they landed, or else they would fall into the hole in the ground. High-voltage wires that surrounded the track were a further complication. The fliers put their heads together and

Handbill headlining Blanche as "The Tomboy of the Air," promoting flying exhibitions in California

FEB. 17. 18. 22. 23. 24. 25

SAT.   SUN.   FRI.   SAT.   SUN.

A THRILL EVERY SECOND

14 Nerve-Tingling, Spine-Chilling, Thrill-Producing Events Every Day. Complete Change of Programme Daily.

RAIN SHINE or CYCLONE

Mail Carrying, Aerial Wireless Telegraphy, Aeroplane Marriage and Honeymoon Trip in the Sky, Etc.

A Monster Flock of World's Greatest Birdmen

MISS BLANCHE SCOTT

REDUCED RAILROAD RATES

ASK YOUR AGENT

"The Tomboy of The Air"

The Most Famous Aviatrix in The World

Watch this daring woman duplicate all the flying tricks of Paulhan

Admission 50 Cents. 2 to 4:30 Daily. For further information address Frank W. Leavitt, Chairman. Room 433 First National Bank Building. Phone Oakland 784.

pooled their experience in order to figure out a way to roll to a stop by making a double S curve. The zigzagging technique usually worked, though half of the team had minor crack-ups. Blanche was fortunate to escape without one. When a major accident did happen, it affected her more than she could have imagined.

When one of the performers, Tom Gunn, came in to land, his touchdown point was too long for him to complete a double S. He made the first S all right, but during the second, one of his wings struck the ground, flipping the plane over and throwing him out of it. A doctor and nurse were always standing by at every meet, and a Red Cross hospital tent was ready for emergencies. Tom was rushed to the tent, but the nurse was nowhere to be found. As the doctor began to set Tom's broken jaw, he pointed to Blanche and directed her to hold the anesthetic cone over Tom's nose. As she assisted, Blanche's beautiful new flying suit became a patchwork of splattered blood from Tom's many injuries.

When Blanche heard the bugle that announced her performance as "the premier aviatrix of the world," there was no time to change her clothes. Fifty thousand people were waiting for her to thrill them with her flying stunts. She didn't disappoint them.

"I was so shook up that I found myself flying with my teeth chattering. The ordeal of the hospital tent, plus the heat, plus the people, plus the ever present fear of the uninsulated high tension wires, topped by a great concern for Tom. Sure I knew he would live but the ordeal was a trying one. I was just plain scared. I knew that before I hung up my goggles, I'd fly other dangerous fields but never was I ever put to the test as I was that day. I gave the customers what they wanted to see. I am sure that you can forgive a pardonable surge of triumph as I came in safely over the wires and made my double 'S' landing safely and perfectly! It was a major triumph of mind and training over shock and emotion!"[4]

"I was so shook up that I found myself flying with my teeth chattering."

Blanche had an accident herself several days later. She had always loved flying tricks, and one of her favorites was flying upside down under bridges. Beachey had been doing a spectacular stunt, and Blanche wanted him to teach it to her. It was a dive. He would take off, circle around until he climbed to nine hundred feet, which was an unusual height, then point the nose of the plane downward and take his foot off the throttle, which plunged the plane into a steep dive. To the spectators, it looked as if the plane was out of control and falling. The propeller turned so slowly, it seemed to be rotating just by the wind, and the crowd couldn't hear the motor that was idling. He held the dive to within fifty feet of the ground, then gunned the motor and pulled out of the dive—to the delight of the audience. The feat kept them coming back to see it again.[5]

Blanche was ready to do the trick, but she observed, "Although the stunt was worth watching more than once, little did the crowd realize that every time it was pulled, the pilot was really taking his life in his own hands."[6]

The first day the Great Western Aerial Circus was booked in Sacramento, Blanche performed the dive stunt, a trick that earned her the honor of being the first woman to stunt-fly. The local newspaper tagged it "the Daring Death Dive," which, naturally, whipped up the expectations of those coming to the show. On the second day, Blanche took off, reached the necessary height, and went into the dive. At the point where she would gun the motor, all she heard was a gurgle—the carburetor had flooded, preventing the motor from starting. Thinking this was very likely to be her real death dive, she quickly began to calculate the length of the plane and the distance to the ground. When she was within ten to twelve feet of the ground, she pulled the nose up sharply, hoping to drag the tail of the plane on the ground enough to come to a stop.

"I dragged the tail all right but the entire rear of the plane cracked up behind me. I got out of what was left, walked over to the inner rail of the track and sat [down], so mad I was bawling my eyes out. Suddenly I was engulfed with a rush of newspaper men and dozens of others who had started on the run toward the wreck. One of the men called out, 'Blanche, Blanche, are you hurt?' 'No I replied,' wiping the tears from my face and brushing wood splinters off my sweater with sharp slapping motions, 'No, I'm not hurt, but would you look at that [darn] machine.'"[7] "I was able to walk away from that landing only because I was wearing my lucky red sweater."[8]

The near misses and crack-ups definitely added to the success of the Great Western Aerial Circus by attracting larger and larger crowds, but it was the pilfering of the proceeds by the promoters that led to the breakup of the circus itself. Everybody quit. Blanche and Glenn Martin returned to building and testing planes. Not long after, they received an offer to be in a meet in Boston. Martin accepted so that he could finance his plane building, and Blanche could never resist the excitement of flying in a meet. Off she went to an aerial show that would end in great tragedy.

Fifteen aviators participated in the event at Squantum Airfield on July 1, 1912, with Blanche and

New England Air Museum, Scott Collection

Posing beside a Curtiss Pusher, Blanche sports her lucky red sweater at the Emeryville Race Track in Oakland, California, February 1912.

Harriet Quimby as the only women. At the time that Blanche was flying over the Aerodrome, the only other plane in the air was Quimby's. Blanche was being careful not to get near the space where Quimby intended to land her plane. Quimby was attempting to fly around Boston Lighthouse, hoping to beat the previous record. The plane she was flying was a 70-horsepower French Blériot two-seater monoplane. It was the most unstable of the Blériot designs because it didn't have ballast, and balance was maintained with a strategically placed bag of sand. William A. P. Willard was in the passenger seat directly behind her. A large man, he was warned to sit perfectly still to maintain the center of gravity, especially since there were no seat belts. When he leaned over to talk to Quimby, the sandbag moved. At two thousand feet, the plane dipped sharply and nose-dived, throwing both Willard and Quimby out of the plane. When they hit the shallow, muddy bay, they were killed instantly. Ironically, the Blériot came out of the dive by itself and landed with very little damage.[9]

Blanche's reaction was quoted in the *New York Evening Journal* two days later. "I saw her head west over Dorchester Bay. Then I saw the crowd rushing down the getaway, and I knew something had happened. I was facing the other way from Miss Quimby at the time, so I did not see the accident, and I am glad that I did not, for I believe it might have unnerved me. I finished a circle of the course and could not land because of the crowd on the getaway." Blanche had to make five circles around the field before the mob was cleared off the landing strip. "It did not dawn on me until I had landed that a serious accident had occurred. . . . It has not discouraged me, although I am slightly unnerved today. I shall continue to fly however. I am the first woman in America to have operated an aeroplane, and I hope to continue until aviation becomes a perfect science."[10] She had landed just as she was running out of gas.

> "He said aviation was for men and that women had no place in it."

Quimby was the first woman to be killed at an aviation meet and the third American woman to lose her life in an airplane. If a man was killed in such an accident, people saw it as bad luck. If a woman died, however, it was said to prove that women could not and should not fly.

One prominent figure who strongly held that opinion was the mayor of Boston, John Fitzgerald. When he summoned Blanche to his office after the tragic accident, she had no idea what to expect. "He told her that women did not possess the tact, judgement, nerve, or ability to meet an unexpected crisis in the air, should one arise. He said aviation was for men and that women had no place in it. He insinuated that neither Quimby's fatal accident nor Blanche's trouble immediately afterward would have happened had a man been at the airplane controls."[11]

True to her nature, Blanche didn't hesitate to tell the mayor emphatically that she absolutely disagreed with him and that women were every bit as efficient as men in piloting airplanes.

Blanche did continue to fly, although Quimby's fatal accident and the recent deaths of Denise Moore and Julia Clarke, just weeks after they received their pilot's licenses, caused Blanche to wonder if her time was running out. Of those four early-flying American women, only Blanche was alive.[12] She had her concerns, but she still had her gumption and grit. Almost one year after the Boston tragedy, her fourth life-threatening episode occurred.

Both Quimby and Blanche had signature flying costumes; Quimby had been known for her purple satin flying suit, and Blanche had her brown satin outfit with helmet and boots. She absolutely banked on the "protection" of her red sweater to keep her from harm.

That was until Memorial Day 1913. She was flying in an air exhibition in Madison, Wisconsin, for the Ward Aviation Company. "It was a warm day and, for the first time I can remember, I didn't wear my lucky red sweater. Just after my first take-off from the fairgrounds, I was climbing and started to make a right-hand turn at about 200 feet when the throttle wire snapped. The torque of the propeller twisted the plane and I dove, nose first, into a swamp at the edge of the field! I was thrown about 30 feet from the plane and broke 41 bones in my body."[13]

The crash broke all of Blanche's ribs, as well as bones in her right hand, forearm, and left elbow. She also smashed her collarbone and right shoulder blade. She was carried onto a Pullman railroad car and routed to a Chicago hospital. She spent eight months recovering in a cast.

One account connected the accident to her not having worn her lucky red sweater, while others reported that Blanche insisted it was sabotage by a rival. She was convinced the crash was not an accident, because the cut on the throttle wire was a clean cut.

Capt. William Winston, who instructed Charles Lindbergh, explains modern flying
instruments to Blanche, 1946.

CHAPTER 6

Ambassador of the Air

T he Wisconsin crash forced Blanche to stop and take stock of her career. The stress from injuries, forty-one broken bones, and her long recovery took a toll on her. She was increasingly bothered by the public's morbid interest in crashes and their disappointment at meets where no one was killed or injured. "Too often people paid money to see me risk my neck, more as a freak—a woman freak pilot—than as a skilled flier."[1] She decided flying was too risky, and she retired from active flying in 1916. She sold her plane, which she had bought to fly in exhibitions at state fairs, to the government to use, as training for World War I was just getting under way. Blanche gave up her career as a pilot, but not her interest in aviation.

Blanche married again and settled in New York City. George Hennings, her millionaire husband, bought her a small motion picture studio on Long Island. She made films for independent producers and the U.S. government. When he died, she moved to

Hollywood, where she worked as a script writer for many major film studios for fourteen years and kept a low profile, at least for Blanche.

In 1930, her mother's ill health brought Blanche back to Rochester, New York. True to her nature and her ability for repartee, she became a local radio personality and talk-show host for many years while caring for her ailing mother.

She wasn't done flying, though, because in 1948, she was invited to the National Air Races in Cleveland on the thirty-eighth anniversary of her solo flight to take a ride in one of the U.S. Air Force's proto-type jet fighters. On September 6, she once again made history, this time by becoming the first American woman to fly in a jet, a TF-80C, piloted by Capt. Chuck Yaeger, the first man to fly faster than the speed of sound. Blanche had added yet another "first" to her list.

A series of events in the 1950s acknowledged Blanche's contribu-tions to aviation. In 1950, a portrait of her was hung in the National Air Museum at the Smithsonian, along with the first airplane to fly and the *Spirit of St. Louis*, Charles Lindbergh's plane. Her portrait was part of a special exhibit commemorating the Early Birds, an organization of pilots who flew before 1916. Blanche was one of only six women. She was also a Hall of Fame member of the OX-5 Club for pilots who flew Curtiss planes with OX-5 engines before January 1, 1941.

In 1953, Blanche was chosen as one of ten American guests of honor, and the only woman, for the National Aeronautical

Blanche holds memorabilia highlighting her flying "firsts."

Organization's special celebration. The occasion was one of several events marking the fiftieth anniversary of the Wright brothers' first flight in 1903. The guests were received by President Dwight D. Eisenhower at the White House, and Blanche was awarded her medal by Gen. James Doolittle in recognition of "real pioneering efforts which have contributed so importantly to the continuing progress of aviation during the first half of the century since Kitty Hawk." The guest list was a roll call of leaders in aviation.

During the 1950s Blanche took up a crusade to preserve and promote the history and contributions of aviation. She was named

public relations consultant for the U.S. Air Force Museum at Wright-Patterson Air Force Base in Dayton, Ohio. She traveled around the country and in Europe, collecting aircraft motors, antique planes, documents, photos, and memorabilia. Among the most valuable items she obtained were fourteen Curtiss-Wright motors used between 1909 and 1914, the plane that Lindbergh flew around the world, and patent designs for a helicopter that were drawn in 1898. She promoted the museum with radio and TV appearances until 1956, having obtained $1,250,000 worth of historical material.

"Women should wake up and take a serious, intelligent, articulate, practical interest in what makes the world tick."

Blanche died on January 12, 1970, leaving a large legacy to aviation.[2] Throughout her career, she lived up to her name of "Tomboy of the Air"; during the course of her life, she was a determined, dynamic individual who made a mark on aviation history and women's accomplishments. She played a major role in attaining credibility for and acceptance of women aviators in a male-dominated field. She was quoted in the *New York Herald* on July 16, 1911: "Women should wake up and take a serious, intelligent, articulate, practical interest in what makes the world tick."[3]

Her lifetime spanned the evolution of aviation into the supersonic age. Airplanes were just being invented when she was born, and she lived to see Neil Armstrong walk on the moon. Her flying accomplishments attest to her courage and ability during a time when none but the best of aviators survived. Her personality and fervor for flying paved the way for other women pilots to test their wings. Adamant that any woman could achieve any personal goal, she was a lady with the courage of her convictions, a woman who dared to live up to her own words. She helped make the world "tick" a little better and faster.

Chronology

The research for this book uncovered many discrepancies in facts, particularly dates. The most disagreement was about when Blanche Stuart Scott was born. She was secretive about her age and known for stretching the truth about it. Even quotes from her do not agree! So I have used the year 1886 as the date given in the most reliable sources.

Reconstructing the life of a person, especially one from a time when historical records were sparse and lacking the precision today's technology makes possible, is a challenge. Every author endeavors to give dimension to the subject of his or her biography and context to that person's world.

The pursuit of information about Blanche and photographs of her and the times was like piecing together a large jigsaw puzzle. The discovery of bits and fragments here and there was due to both serendipity and librarians' logic. One of the thrills was finding segments from Blanche's personal scrapbooks at the New England Air Museum (Windsor Locks, Conn.). Their treasure trove of files contained crumbling newspaper clippings and photographs that Blanche herself pasted onto the pages; they added luster to her personality and accentuated her determination.

Of the more than thirty photos that I found, many were unsuitable for reproduction. Some of the ones we chose to include in the book are not crystal clear, but we felt they conveyed the vivacity, zeal, and daring of this era of early aviation.

Blanche was a genuine character, and she became real to me. I hope she will be to the reader as well.

April 8, 1886	Born in Rochester, New York.
May 16, 1910	Began a historic cross-country automobile trip.
July 23, 1910	Completed the trip and became the first woman to drive an automobile cross-country from New York City to San Francisco.
August 1910	Arrived at the Glenn Curtiss Flying School and became the first and only woman to be taught to fly by Glenn H. Curtiss.
August 18, 1910	Her first flight, when plane lifted off the ground.
September 2, 1910	Her first solo flight. Became first woman pilot in United States.

October 23, 1910	Flew in an air meet in Fort Wayne, Indiana; made the first public flight by a woman in the United States.
Summer 1911	Performed the lead role in first silent movie about flying, *The Aviator's Bride,* filmed at Mineola Field, Long Island, New York.
Summer 1911	Flew the first long-distance flight by a woman, from Mineola to Central Islip, Long Island, New York—a total distance of sixty miles.
1912	Became first woman test pilot, Griffith Park, California.
1912	First woman stunt flier.
1916	Retired from active flying.
September 6, 1948	First American woman to fly in a jet; plane was piloted by Capt. Charles (Chuck) Yaeger in a TF-80C at the National Air Races, Cleveland, Ohio.
July 1950	Her portrait was hung in National Air Museum, Washington, D.C.
October 14, 1953	National Aeronautics Association sponsored celebration for fiftieth anniversary of powered flight at the White House. The event honored pioneers in the development of aviation, and Blanche was a guest of honor.
1953–1958	She worked for the United States Air Force Museum in Dayton, Ohio. In her role as public relations consultant, she acquired materials relating to early flight for the museum's collection—$1,250,000 worth of antique planes, photos, and memorabilia.
1956	Made honorary member of Flying Red Cross Nurses.
February 7, 1960	Antique Airplane Association honored the fiftieth anniversary of Scott's first flight at an event in New York City.
January 12, 1970	Died. Many newspapers said she was eighty-four.
December 20, 1980	Scott was honored with a U.S. Postal Service issue of a special commemorative stamp. Glenn Curtiss was honored at the same time. It was one more "first" for her, the first time two commemorative stamps were issued on the same day.

Notes

1. SPEED AND BALANCE

1. Norman E. Borden, Jr., "The Aviators" (unpublished manuscript), 171.

2. Ibid.

3. Blanche Stuart Scott (as told to William J. Adams), "Not on a Broom" (unpublished manuscript), 4.

2. OVER LAND IN AN OVERLAND

1. Scott, "Not on a Broom," 7.

2. Henry Ford built his first car in 1892, and the first Model T was completed in 1908. By 1920, there were 8 million automobiles rattling around on America's rutted roads. In contrast to Blanche's Lady Overland, the Model T cost only three hundred dollars, enabling many Americans to afford a car. Ten years after Blanche's trip, cars were reshaping everyday life.

3. *Democrat and Chronicle* (Rochester, New York), June 2, 1946.

4. William J. Adams, "Rochester's Remarkable Flying Redhead!" (unpublished article), 2.

5. Scott, "Not on a Broom," 16.

6. Ibid., 14.

3. UP IN THE AIR

1. Scott, "Not on a Broom," 23.

2. Ibid.

3. The Wright brothers had obtained a patent on a method of twisting wings to control flight. They claimed that Curtiss's ailerons, the hinged flaps on the wings that he had designed, violated their patent. They won a court case against Curtiss, making the rivalry even more fierce.

4. Fran Walosin, "Blanche Stuart Scott: First Lady of American Aviation," *Wingspan*, August 1959, 7.

5. Ibid.

6. Marcia Gitelman, "Blanche Stuart Scott: America's First Aviatrix," *Woman Pilot*, March/April 1998, 20.

7. Scott, "Not on a Broom," 30.

8. Ibid., 34.

9. Gitelman, "Blanche Stuart Scott," 20.

10. IIbid., 21.

11. Ibid.

12. Henry M. Holden, with Captain Lori Griffith, *Ladybirds: The Untold Story of Women Pilots in America* (Mt. Freedom, New Jersey: Black Hawk Publishing Company, 1991), 16.

13. Ibid., 17.

14. Ibid., 17.

15. Gitelman, "Blanche Stuart Scott," 21.

16. Scott, "Not on a Broom," 47.

17. Ibid.

18. Ibid., 48.

4. FLYING HIGH AND FAR

1. Scott, "Not on a Broom," 50.

2. Amelia Bloomer was the nineteenth-century feminist who advocated pants for women in 1851. Named after her, "bloomers" were intended to replace heavy dresses with tight waists and hoop skirts to give women freedom of movement.

3. Gitelman, "Blanche Stuart Scott," 21.

4. Matilde Moisant flew a Blériot plane named *Lucky Thirteen*, after her favorite number. She was flying in a show in Dallas, Texas, when the fuel tank developed a leak and the plane burst into flames when she landed. She miraculously escaped. Her heavy tweed flying suit saved her from being critically burned. That flight ended her career.

5. What tipped the decision to award Glenn Curtiss the first license issued by the Aero Club of America was based on his being the first American to make a public flight in the United States. The key word is *public*, as the Wright brothers' initial flights were not. On July 4, 1908, Curtiss flew just over a mile in an airplane built by members of the Aerial Experiment Association.

6. Edward R. Cowles, "Tomboy of the Air," *UA Beehive*, Summer 1968, 18.

7. In addition to Quimby becoming the first licensed American woman pilot on August 1, 1911, she made another historic mark by becoming the first woman to fly across the English Channel on April 16, 1912. Because the ship *Titanic* sank the day before her flight, there were no headlines of her achievement.

8. Scott, "Not on a Broom," 56.

9. Ibid., 59.

10. Ibid., 60.

11. Ibid.

12. Ibid., 60–61.

13. Borden, "The Aviators," 291.

14. Scott, "Not on a Broom," 73.

15. Ibid., 74–75.

16. Fran Walosin, "Blanche Stuart Scott," *Wingspan,* October 1959, 10.

17. Scott, "Not on a Broom," 81.

18. Ibid., 95.

19. Ibid.

4. CIRCUS IN THE AIR

1. Scott, "Not on a Broom," 98.

2. Ruth Law made many aviation records. In 1913, she flew a moonlit flight around Staten Island, making her the first woman to fly at night. In 1915, she performed the first loop-the-loop stunt in an acrobatic exhibition in Daytona Beach, Florida. In 1916, she attempted to fly from Chicago to New York City in one day. Though she failed to make the distance in that time, she set an American nonstop cross-country flying record of 590 miles. The record held for one year.

3. Scott, "Not on a Broom," 107.

4. Ibid., 119.

5. Ibid., 122.

6. Ibid.

7. Ibid., 123.

8. Borden, "The Aviators," 328.

9. Ironically, another aviatrix was in the audience that day and saw the accident—Ruth Law.

10. *New York Evening Journal,* July 13, 1912.

11. Borden, "The Aviators," 341.

12. Denise Moore was killed on July 21, 1911, three weeks after receiving her pilot's license. Julia Clarke was flying in an exhibition at the Illinois State Fair when her plane clipped a tree and she was killed, just twenty-nine days after she received her license, on June 17, 1912.

13. Borden, "The Aviators," 357–358.

6. AMBASSADOR OF THE AIR

1. Holden, *Ladybirds,* 17.

2. The December 25, 1948, issue of *Collier's* magazine called Blanche's solo flight—she being the first woman in America to fly—the third-most-important event in American aviation. The first event was the Wright brothers' flight and second was the sending of the first message by wireless telegraphy from J. A. D. McCurdy to radio engineer Harry Horton at Sheepshead Bay, New York, on August 27, 1910.

3. *New York Herald,* July 16, 1911.

Bibliography

Adams, Bill. "Blanche Stuart Scott: An Affectionate Farewell." *Aviation Travel*, March/April 1993.

———. "Blanche Scott." *Upstate*, Rochester, New York: *Democrat and Chronicle*, December 4, 1969.

Adams, William J. "Rochester's Remarkable Flying Redhead!" Unpublished article, Curtiss Museum, Hammondsport, New York.

Borden, Norman E., Jr. "The Aviators." Unpublished manuscript, New England Air Museum, Windsor Locks, Connecticut.

Cowles, Edward R. "Tomboy of the Air." *UA Beehive*, Summer 1968.

Gitelman, Marcia. "Blanche Stuart Scott: America's First Aviatrix." *Woman Pilot*, March/April 1998.

Holden, Henry M., with Captain Lori Griffith. *Ladybirds: The Untold Story of Women Pilots in America.* Mt. Freedom, New Jersey: Black Hawk Publishing Company, 1991.

Sayers, Edwin. "On the Road, In the Air." *Upstate*, Rochester, New York: *Democrat and Chronicle*, July 6, 1980.

Scott, Blanche Stuart (as told to William J. Adams). "Not on a Broom." Unpublished manuscript, National Air and Space Museum, Washington, D.C.

Stickler, Merrill. "Blanche Stuart Scott, 1886–1970." Unpublished article, Curtiss Museum, Hammondsport, New York.

Walosin, Fran. "Blanche Stuart Scott: First Lady of American Aviation." *Wingspan*, July, August, September, and October 1959; January 1960.

Index

$16.95

DATE			

SEP   2001